How George Throckmorton Unmasked Mark Hofmann's Forgeries

(Note this conversation was recorded on August 11, 2017 in Taylorsville, Utah. I will use GT for Gospel Tangents to indicate when I am talking to George. The interview has been lightly edited to remove verbal miscues.)

Introduction

Welcome to Gospel Tangents, the best source for Mormon history, science, and theology. I'm your host Rick Bennett. Please consider donating or purchasing a transcript by going to our website https://GospelTangents.com/shop . You'll help support other documentaries and podcasts such as this.

George Throckmorton is one of the most amazing police officers in the world. Last year I talked to him about his role in the Mark Hofmann forgeries and bombings. He will talk about the methods he used to discover how Mark Hofmann was forging documents using a toy chemistry set! We'll discuss George's interactions with the FBI, interviews with prosecutors and key witnesses, and George's interactions with LDS Church leaders, including Elder Dallin Oaks tremendous help in unmasking Mark Hofmann. Check out our conversation....

Contents

Tags: George Throckmorton, Rick Bennett, Gospel Tangents, Mark Hofmann, forgery, murder, Howard Hughes will, sports memorabilia, Hi-Fi Murders, Mormon Will, Dale Pierre, FBI, BATF, Alcohol Tobacco and Firearms, toy chemistry set, Gordon B. Hinckley, Dallin Oaks, Salamander Letter, 60 Minutes, document examiner, LDS secret vaults, cracked ink, sports forgeries, Brent Ashworth, Brent Metcalfe, Lyn Jacobs, pipe bomb, Mike Hansen, Steve Christensen, Kathy Sheets, Oath of a Freeman, Massachusetts Bay Colony , Schiller and Wapner, Brent Ashworth, William McLellin, McLellin Collection, Hugh Pinnock, Dallin Oaks, Gordon Hinckley, First Interstate Bank, Spaulding Theory, Martin Harris, Solomon Spaulding, death penalty, plea bargain,

George Throckmorton on Hi-Fi/ Hofmann Forgeries/Murders

Introduction

George Throckmorton is one of the most amazing police officers in the world. Last year I talked to him about his role in the Mark Hofmann forgeries and bombings. In this first episode, we'll get acquainted with him, and learn how he became a forgery expert. Of course, we will talk about the Mark Hofmann forgeries and murders, but we will also briefly discuss one of his first forgery cases in Ogden, Utah. The Hi-Fi Shop murders are well-known in Utah because a few robbers tortured and robbed an Ogden store called the Hi-Fi Shop. It turns out that forgery was involved in that case! Check out our conversation.....

GT: <u>00:00:56</u>   Welcome to *Gospel Tangents podcast*. I'm really excited to meet with George Throckmorton. George worked with the Salt Lake City Police Department. Is that right?

George: <u>00:01:06</u>   I worked for many agencies over a period of 40 years. I retired from the Salt Lake City Police Department.

GT: <u>00:01:12</u>   Okay, so you have the claim to fame of figuring out how Mark Hofmann was doing his forgeries. So, I'm really excited to talk about how all that happened and all that process. So, can you tell us a little bit about your background? How did you get into document examining?

George: 00:01:36   Document examining was quite by accident quite frankly. I got out of high school and joined the army and got into the military police. When I was going through their training there, I realized I liked more of the scientific aspects than the rough and tumble of the streets that is going on. When I got home off of my mission for the church, I got married. About two years after that, then we moved to Ogden. At the time I was an insurance investigator and I got transferred to Ogden. While there I got on the Ogden Police Department and after about two and a half years I decided I wanted to get into the crime lab. So, there was some, at that time actually a home study course you took for all the aspects of forensics. It wasn't called forensics back then, but it is now. And for a while, and this was with no college, and so I started working in the crime lab and then I thought I needed more training, so I started going to Weber State which had one of the first five police science departments in the United States and I found I enjoyed it.

George: 00:02:53   Later on I had the opportunity to go back to Chicago and teach at the Institute of Applied Science, which was the oldest forensic school in the world at the time and while I was there, my areas of expertise was to be fingerprints and handwriting identification and that's when I was actually introduced into handwriting identification, which is the main focus of document examination. I stayed in Chicago for a year, didn't want to raise my son in Chicago. We were living on the 17th floor of an apartment house downtown Chicago, and he enjoyed throwing water balloons out the window. We decided we needed to get back home, so we left and came back to Ogden. I was rehired on the police department, immediately assigned to the crime lab. The document examiner we had had retired and so they asked me to start doing the work, which I did, so that's a long story to explain how I got into it.

George: 00:03:54 Since then I received a lot of training over the years and the training to be a document examiner is actually 4,160 hours. Since I'm not doing it full time. It took me about 10 years to get the training before I met the minimum qualifications to be a document examiner and eventually it turned into a full-time profession.

GT: 00:04:16 Wow. That's amazing. Now you grew up in, or I guess you didn't grow up in Ogden, but were you there? I know Ogden's been a little bit notorious with these Hi-Fi Murders.[1] Did you have anything on that?

George: 00:04:26 Yes, that was my investigation. I processed that scene.

GT: 00:04:30 Oh Wow. That was an awful murder.

George: 00:04:30 It was awful.

GT: 00:04:34 So I don't know how many of my listeners are familiar with a Hi-Fi Murders as they were known, but there were some criminals that tortured

---

[1] For basic introduction, see https://en.wikipedia.org/wiki/Hi-Fi_murders

some people and killed them. It was pretty terrible.

George: 00:04:49   Ironically that case, a significant part of that was due to handwriting.

GT: 00:04:52   Really? Oh, I didn't know that.

George: 00:04:55   Again, we could go into that and I don't want to take a lot of time because that's not the emphasis.

GT: 00:04:59   I'll have to come back. We'll have to talk about that.

George: 00:05:04   The significance was there was a homicide up there before the Hi-Fi Shop Murders, there was a homicide involving in airman from Hill Air Force Base and there was an auto theft ring going on out of Hill Air Force Base and they would steal cars and get an airman that was being released and asked him if he wanted to earn some extra money and he would drive the car back to the Chicago/Detroit area so he would get paid. And he was actually transporting stolen cars. But they didn't know it.

GT: 00:05:04   Oh my.

George: 00:05:34   This one fellow had a car that Dale Pierre [wanted. He] is the one that did the killings in the Hi-Fi Shop case. Dale Pierre had Sunday lunch with this man. He says, "I want to buy your car." And the guy says, "I don't want to sell it," because they were actually taking orders for certain types of cars.

GT: 00:05:34 Oh my goodness.

George: 00:05:57 And so they watched the football game. The guy went to sleep on the couch and Pierre stabbed him 10-12 times with an ice pick and killed him and stole his car. In order for the cars to go back east, they had to have two sets of keys and Pierre can only find one set of keys. So, he went out to the base and got a duplicate set of keys made. He had to sign for that. I actually was able to attach his signature to request for the extra set of keys on that investigation when the Hi-Fi Shop Murders happened. So, we had been investigating that already and he was a suspect in that murder.

GT: 00:06:35 Oh, so, it was a completely different murder. Wow.

George: 00:06:39 Yes. And then later on, some evidence developed out of the Hill Air Force Base, we went on a search warrant in the dumpsters out there and the detective with the auto theft and myself were in the dumpsters. We found the identification of the victims and he stopped, he looked up and he says, "Dale Pierre's room is right over there," and that's how Dale Pierre became a suspect. We went over and got a search warrant a few days later and, we found a contract hidden underneath his carpet for a storage unit. And in the storage unit was all of the equipment that was taken out of the Hi-Fi Shop.

GT: 00:06:39   Oh my goodness.

George: 00:07:18   So in a nutshell, that's how things happened on that.

GT: 00:07:23   Wow. I will bet you have a lot of stories to tell.

George: 00:07:26   Over the years, it's extremely interesting to find out. So many cases, big cases have evidence stemming from handwriting identification or document examination, but the Hofmann case that we're talking about was the largest, and actually the biggest in the world in the history that was voted on by several document examination groups.

GT: 00:07:50   Wow, that's amazing. So, how did you get involved with the Hofmann case?

George: 00:08:00   The Hofmann case was quite by accident. I was working for the Attorney General's office as a white-collar investigator at the time, special agent for them. And the bombs went off in Salt Lake and we were specifically told to stay out of the investigation because of the high profile that was going on with various agencies. The FBI; Alcohol, Tobacco and Firearms was involved; the county sheriff was involved. Salt Lake Police was involved, and the attorney general says, "Stay out of it." So, I did.

George: 00:08:33   But because I had worked at the state crime laboratory prior to going into the attorney general's office. The news media was aware that I was the only document examiner in Utah and they kept calling me about the authenticity of the *Salamander Letter*. And all I was allowed to say at that time was, "I've never seen the *Salamander Letter*, so I can't discuss it."

George: <u>00:08:58</u> Later on because of publicity or pressure, I don't know, the attorney general says, "well you can talk about it in a generic point of view, making sure to tell them that we're not involved." So, I did that. And then along the way I got contacted. The news media called me from all over the country and the state and the city and so forth. And that's what I told them. And then, it was actually about six weeks later before I got involved, after the bombings, before I actually got involved and it was quite by accident because Dean Jessee, who was a historian and professor, I don't know exactly what he did, he called me and asked me if I would look at the *Salamander Letter*, a picture of it.

GT: <u>00:09:43</u> Oh, so it wasn't the police that got you involved. It was a historian.

George: <u>00:09:45</u> Correct. I was doing that strictly as a favor to him because he asked me to do it and I met with him and he showed me a copy of it and I was intrigued by it.

George: <u>00:09:55</u> And I was also surprised and intrigued by who had an authenticated it because Dean told me, he says, "I'm really not a document examiner. I'm just familiar with people's writing and I can tell you who supposedly wrote it."

George: 00:10:09   I asked him at the time, "Well, how do you know it's not forged?"

George: 00:10:14   And he made the comment to me, "Who would want to forge a historical document?"

George: 00:10:21   Well, I knew who, because that was my profession. But it was not his. Working for the church, I think they have a tendency to believe everybody is honest. Working for law enforcement, I have a tendency to believe everybody's crooked and so it takes somewhere in the middle to find the truth sometimes. And so, I looked at it and I realized the person that authenticated it, lived in Boston and he represented himself as being the best document examiner in the world.

George: 00:10:46   And as I started doing some research on him, I found out he was a book dealer. He owned a bookshop in Boston and none of the people in the organizations, the scientists, if I can use that term, was aware of him at all. It's a totally different branch of civilization or science or whatever you want to call it. And I noticed in reading the report he wrote, when he authenticated it, there were some scientific errors in his assumption. And in reading an article about him in *Newsweek* magazine, there were some additional statements he made that were not scientifically accurate. And so, then I started telling everybody, "Nobody has ever authenticated the *Salamander Letter*." And our job at the attorney general's office was to assist other law enforcement agencies. And

there's politics involved here because Ted Cannon
was the district attorney at that time.

George: 00:11:51   I daresay he was the most powerful Democrat in
the State of Utah. He had recommended the
attorney general for his position and
coincidentally the attorney general got that
position.

GT: 00:11:51   Oh, wow.

George: 00:12:05   I mean, so there's some politics going on, which,
as there always are in any political arena. There's
a lot of that that goes on. But anyway, Ted
Cannon finally took over the investigation
because there were so many different agencies
and his thoughts were, "We're going to be the
ones prosecuting it, so we're going to do the
investigation." So, he set up a team. There were
two from the Salt Lake Police Department, which
were assigned to investigate the homicides. There
were two from the district attorney's office that
was there to investigate the fraud. And then there
were other people coming in to assist in various
areas and he requested, the attorney general,
asked if I could come down and assist with the
investigation.

George: 00:12:53   He did that only after I was through talking to
Dean Jessee and I had the *Salamander Letter*. I
had a few other copies of letter, which Dean
provided me and he's really a key to this whole
thing. His cooperation and his access to
documents in history. And I was looking at this
handwriting once and I was looking at a

12

document that was supposedly the last letter ever written by Joseph Smith while he was in the Carthage Jail, just in fact less than an hour before he was killed. And it was a letter which was addressed to General Dunham. It said, "Come and break me out of jail. I'm tired of being here." Now realize I'm paraphrasing because I don't know the exact words. Well, this contradicts history. From what I had heard, I had heard Joseph Smith had resigned himself to die. Now he's telling them to bring out the Nauvoo militia and break me out of jail.

George: 00:13:48   But as I was looking, I was sitting down and doing some hard labor in my reclining chair watching a television show because I would look at these documents for frequently two or three hours and I started noticing some inconsistencies and I called Dean Jessee on the phone and I says, "Dean," I says, "I'm looking at this document. I think I found a $3 bill."

George: 00:13:48   To me he said, "They don't make $3 bills."

George: 00:14:15   Ironically later on I found that Hofmann did make some $3 bills.

GT: 00:14:15   Oh, that's funny.

George: 00:14:20   But anyway, so at that time I realized something was wrong and I called the district attorney's office Monday morning because I had worked with them when I was working at the crime laboratory and so forth. And I talked to the investigator I knew, and I says," I think there may be some forgeries involved in this investigation." Now this is six weeks after the bombing.

George: 00:14:40   And they had no idea there was any forgeries. He said, "Could you come down and meet with us tomorrow morning?"

George: 00:14:45   So I went down there and I sat down and met with the district attorney and two of the investigators and one of the attorneys, and I told them my suspicions. The problem they were having is they knew Mark Hofmann made the bombs. They knew that within 12 hours of the bombs. We're now six weeks later, they had no idea why, because all of the documents had been authenticated and when I told them I suspected forgery at that time, they were quite elated. In fact, I was told by one of the investigators after we left the interview, he walked down the hall to go back to his office, jumped up in the air and clicked his heels together and says, "We got it!"

George: 00:15:28   And so that's how I got involved originally. And then I became part of the team. So, we met together every morning and discussed what was going on. The assignments were made to the various people. My job was to look at the documents and then so I was interacting with the various investigators and so I got to hear kind of the complete story.

GT: 00:15:50   Wow. Yeah, that's, that's really interesting. I didn't realize it had taken so long for them to figure out a motive. So, it was you that basically came up with a motive then?

George: 00:15:50   That's correct.

GT: 00:15:50   Wow. That's interesting.

George: 00:16:00   They had no idea. In fact, we wanted to have a
                     search warrant to go out and look for stuff in
                     Hofmann's house, but they thought we cannot do
                     it. We've already had two search warrants at his
                     house. Unfortunately for them, the search
                     warrants were to look for bomb apparatus, not
                     forgery apparatus, and they was afraid that the
                     news media would really attack them viciously for
                     going out a third time because already even
                     people in my old ward, my home teacher and a
                     friend, "You're on the wrong path. You're talking
                     to the wrong person. He's innocent. You're trying
                     to frame him." And we're just getting that from
                     the news media all of the time.

How Hofmann Fooled Experts with a Toy Chemistry Set

Introduction

We're continuing our discussion with George Throckmorton. He is the expert who discovered how Mark Hofmann was forging documents. Did you know that Mark actually used a toy chemistry set? It's pretty amazing. We will also discuss George's role in the famous Howard Hughes will. (Is there anything this guy wasn't involved with?) It's really interesting. Check out our conversation.....

GT: 00:16:38 So how would you go about trying to find out if a document had been forged? It just looked similar to someone's handwriting versus was legitimately their handwriting. How would you figure that out?

George: 00:16:48 Well, there's many techniques and that's why it takes 4,000 hours of training to do it. It's not like you see on television where they pick it up in two minutes. They give you a total description. The other thing that's a problem is there's two branches of science that examine handwriting, and the public doesn't understand that at all. One of them is called graphology. That's where they do the personality assessment of a person's writing. In fact, the Howard Hughes will, that was the big, if they remember the Howard Hughes will. He was the richest man in the world at the time and when they found the will, which they call the Mormon will, I don't know how much you're familiar with this story.

GT: 00:17:25   We might have to schedule another interview.

George: 00:17:31   Well, I got involved in that quite by accident.

GT: 00:17:31   Really?

George: 00:17:31   Yes.

GT: 00:17:31   Oh my goodness.

George: 00:17:31   See I have been involved in basically many, many high profile cases in Utah and around the country because of the way these things work out.

GT: 00:17:40   We're going to have to have another interview.

George: 00:17:44   But anyway, that testimony in court on Howard Hughes will, was a result of having the graphologists testifying against the document examiners.

GT: 00:17:52   Oh my goodness.

George: 00:17:53   Because they'll say, well, Howard Hughes would put a counterclockwise hook on his lower letter g, which means he has back problems. Howard Hughes did have back problems, so that's him. That's graphology.

GT: 00:17:53   Wow.

George: 00:18:07   He'll tell you your personality and that's something that's not valid in the field of documents. An average examination of a signature. For me it's just an average signature is one to three hours and there's so many factors. I use 21 different tests on a signature before I examine it. If you look at a document, you're looking at a whole lot more and it's kind of interesting. The Salamander Letter, because so many people had authenticated it, including the FBI eventually got it and they authenticated it. So, when I was examining it, I spent 100 hours on a one-page document looking at everything I could think of from water stains, to marks on the paper, to erasures, to deletions, to chemical treatment, to handwriting itself, to the ink that was used, the pressure that was exerted, stuff like this. It's a very difficult examination to do. That's why in the United States there's about 300-400 is all, documents examiners in the whole United States and Canada that do the work.

GT: 00:19:11   Wow, That's crazy. So, when you looked at the *Salamander Letter*, what was kind of the giveaway on that? What wasn't legitimate?

George: 00:19:19   There wasn't no giveaway on that. In fact, the *Salamander Letter* was not examined until about four or five weeks after I started examining documents.

GT: 00:19:34   So we're two or three months out now, from the bombing.

George: 00:19:36   Yes. The bombing took place October 15th and we're into February or March before I even get the *Salamander Letter* because the FBI got it.

GT: <u>00:19:50</u>   Oh, so now let's double check there because you said it was about six weeks after Dean Jessee had let you see the *Salamander Letter*?

George: <u>00:19:50</u>   That's correct.

GT: <u>00:19:57</u>   Okay. And then from there it went to the FBI?

George: <u>00:20:01</u>   Well, I never saw the original document. I saw a photograph of the *Salamander Letter* from Dean, but in the process of doing that initial examination for him, it was not the *Salamander Letter* that tipped me off. It was that other letter, which was the *General Dunham letter* that was the one I was concerned with. We met with representatives of the church, the attorney and myself did. We met with the attorney of the church. Now attorneys are different than the representatives of the church and there was quite an antagonistic meeting at that time. We had two of the representatives of the church there, one that was helping to run the library and we went in and we requested. We said we were investigating a possible forgery. We need some documents that Hofmann had that are in your possession. We need the original documents and we want to examine them to see if there's forgeries.

George: <u>00:21:00</u>   We haven't even talked about *Salamander Letter* yet. Okay. We're talking about these others because the church never had the *Salamander Letter* at that time. And so, I remember well and it's not very flattering, but I remember well the attorney for the church at that time would pound his hand on the desk when we would ask for something. He says, "It's my job to protect the President Hinckley and protect the church. You cannot have these documents."

George: 00:21:29   And we would talk and the attorney for the district attorney's office would talk. I basically watched and he said, "But this is a homicide investigation. We need these documents." And we were meeting them for at least 20 to 25 minutes with him pounding his hand on that desk at least five to six different times. And he said, okay.

George: 00:21:51   And the representatives from the church says, "There's nothing secret about these documents. They've been published. They are in magazines. There's photographs of them. They can have them."

George: 00:22:01   "It's my job to protect President Hinckley and protect the church."

George: 00:22:06   Finally I got disgusted and I got up and walked out while he's in there. When the attorney for the district attorney's office come running after me and says, "George, You gotta come back. We got to get these documents for our investigation."

George: 00:22:19   And as bullheaded as I was at the time, I says, "I don't report to you. I worked for the Attorney General's office, not you guys." And I says, "I'm not going to deal with anybody like this. This is a homicide case." So, I left. I got a call about two or three or four days later, something like that.

George: 00:22:39   He says, "We're going to be meeting with Elder Dallin Oaks." He was a former Supreme Court justice. He's a lawyer, BYU president.

George: 00:22:46   He knows the law, so I thought maybe we can talk to him. Plus, he's an apostle. That helps. We walked in and sat down with him and explained what happened and he was not pleased with what had previously happened. He actually stood up and he looked at me and he said, "You will have the total and complete cooperation of the church. And he turned to me and he says, "If there is anybody that is not cooperating with you, you let me know personally." And from then on, the doors were open. We got anything I wanted. I got to go into what was affectionately called the super-secret vaults of the church and they're really not that big. It's not that impressive. It is impressive, but they're not that secret. But some of the other people say they are. But anyway, I got to go anyplace I want to do anything I wanted and that really turned the investigation around because now a forensic examination of document means you have to compare a genuine document with something else, another document, and it's through the comparison of these known documents to the questioned document to see if it's genuine or not. Is it the same type of paper, the same type of ink, the same writing, same circumstances of being stored? All of these things are a factor in it. But that was what actually changed the investigation around.

GT: 00:24:19   So Elder Oaks was really helpful to allowing more access.

George: 00:24:21 Absolutely. There was no question. I had a lot of respect for him before, but I had even more respect after meeting with him in that meeting. He wasn't happy. In fact, ironically, I heard, and remember this was 30 years ago, so my memory's not exactly as sharp as it was, but they dismissed the whole law firm that had been with the church for years and they got a new one.

GT: 00:24:21 Oh really?

George: 00:24:44 I understood it was because of that, but that's just my own understanding. Take it for what it's worth.

GT: 00:24:50 That's interesting.

George: 00:24:51 All I know is there was a change in law firm shortly thereafter.

GT: 00:24:55 That's very interesting. So, it was this Jonathan Dunham letter that kind of tipped you off a little bit. What were some things that you thought because originally, I guess you just saw a photograph, but there were some things there that, that tipped you off?

George: 00:25:08 That's correct. It was actually a Xerox copy, but the one thing I noticed on the *General Dunham letter* was there was two different pens used and the paper had three things on the side of it which indicated it was torn out of a book.

GT: 00:25:08 Oh.

George: 00:25:28   And I'm looking just logically for no other reason other than a gut feeling. I'm thinking "Here's some people, Joseph and Hyrum, and a couple of others in Carthage Jail. How many writing instruments would they have access to there? How many different types of paper would they have access to? Because I've got other--Dean provided me with other letters from Carthage Jail that were written while they were in jail. So, I'm comparing the other letters that were written to this General Dunham letter. Now it certainly is possible that they had to use a different paper and they had to use a different pen, but I'm thinking, "Why? You're in jail? Do they give you a sample of pens?" That was my suspicions right there and I could see the two different pens were involved between them.

George: 00:26:12   I had two or three letters from the jail and so it's just a gut feeling, but before I could do an examination, I needed the original and that's why I called them and says "There's a suspicion. There may be some forgeries." I wasn't certain by any means. In fact, when I started doing the investigation, I called a document examiner friend of mine in Phoenix. You might find this interesting. His name is Bill Flynn. When I first got hired at the crime laboratory in 1981 in Utah, I went down to Phoenix and I worked with him and several others in the state crime laboratory down there. Bill is from Philadelphia and he's, in my opinion, he's probably the foremost document examiner in the country. He's very intelligent and perceptive and so forth, and I got the chance to work with them down there for two weeks.

George: 00:27:03   I realized I'm in a can of hot water here because I'm a Mormon. These are Mormon documents. If I say they're forgeries, "You're just saying that because you're a Mormon." If I say they're genuine, "Oh, you're just saying that because you're a Mormon." I needed to find somebody else. I called Bill on the phone and I thought it was funny. I called him, and he answered the phone. I says, "Hi, Bill. This is George.

George: 00:27:27   "Oh, hi. How are you doing?"

George: 00:27:27   I says, "What religion are you?"

George: 00:27:32   He kind of paused. "Well, I'm Catholic, but I'm not active."

George: 00:27:32   I says, "Good."

George: 00:27:32   Then he said, "What's going on?"

George: 00:27:39   And I told him I had this investigation. So, he helped me from there on, for the next six months. He actually came up and spent two or three weeks with me working on some of the documents here. The rest of the time he was in Phoenix doing his regular job. In addition, he was doing other things. So, we communicated about every day for six months. I was working on part of the case, part of the evidence. He was working on other elements. Can I tell a sidelight, a little story again?

GT   00:27:39   Yes, go ahead. We're the *Gospel Tangents*. We can go off on tangents.

George: 00:28:17   Oh, good. He was working on the ink and he got some old ink recipes and we had a problem with how to make the ink because what we're trying to do is duplicate the Hofmann documents and he was working on the ink.

George: 00:28:31   I was working on other aspects of the paper and other things. But, anyway, he looked in some old history books and found some ink formulas for the ink that was used at that time, in the 1830s, and so forth. And it was basically iron gallotannic ink that was used. They told how to make the ink. They had the formula. There was green copperas, Roman vitriol and gum Arabic and other things like that. And so, he went out and we tried to find these chemicals and I tried to help him with that. And we contacted the chemists at the lab, Ph.D. chemists and we contacted the chemists at the universities, and so they'd never heard of these chemicals. And anyway, so he made some, which he thought were comparable to some of these other things, but we couldn't find gum Arabic and we looked everywhere.

George: 00:29:29   Gum Arabic is a thickening substance. They use in soft drinks and gravies and stuff like that. So. it's out there, but where do we buy it? And more importantly, where it would Mark Hofmann buy it? Finally, he says, "You know, my brother works the Food and Drug Administration in Washington, D.C. He just got hired there about two or three months ago. Maybe I ought to give him a call." So as Bill related the story to me, he says, "I called him up, I hadn't seen him for a long time," and they talked for a few minutes. And he says, "Well, the reason I'm calling, I wonder if you could help me. I'm trying to find some gum Arabic." He said there was a silence on the phone.

George: 00:30:06   He says, "Why do you need gum Arabic?

George: 00:30:07   And he says, "We're involved in investigation." And he said, "It's interesting you asked. I have been assigned to be in charge of all the gum Arabic. I'm looking at it right now in the library. Every publication that's ever been printed on Gum Arabic? What do you need?"

GT: 00:30:07   Wow.

George: 00:30:28   So it's, you know, it's a coincidence as some people say. That's what Bill said. He said, "Isn't that a coincidence?" But anyway, that's a side light on that.

GT: 00:30:28   What is gum Arabic? Does it have a different name now or...?

George: 00:30:41   No, it's still called gum Arabic. In fact, later on we made some ink. He did. Bill did, that worked. And we found out, and I was looking at how did they artificially age it and so forth. And between the two of us, we found out that you can artificially age iron gallotannic ink by several different methods. An easy one is simply put it in the oven because it accelerates the heat process and the aging process. And Mark tried that on some of them, by the way. He experimented with several different forms of doing it until they found the

one that was easiest and most popular, which
was a chemical treatment.

George: 00:31:22   But anyway, and we finally found the chemicals
and the chemicals we found over a year after the
bombs. It was in November of 1986. The bombs
were in October of '85 and I was out Christmas
shopping in a toy store and happened to glance
down to the toy chemistry set. And right there
was gum Arabic, Roman vitriol, green copperas,
and a recipe on how to make iron gallotannic ink.

GT: 00:31:22   No way, that's crazy.

George: 00:31:50   Later on we found out that's where he got the
chemicals was at a toy store.

GT: 00:31:50   At a toy store.

George: 00:31:55   And yet they fooled the biggest laboratory in the
world, the FBI.

GT: 00:31:55   So yeah, that's crazy.

George: 00:32:03   They were looking for a more sophisticated way
of doing things today than what he used. He used
method that was used 150 years ago. And we
don't deal with things 150 years old. We deal with
modern, at the time forgeries on checks and stuff
like that, credit applications. And we're very
proficient at that, but even in the field of
document examination, we couldn't go to
anybody to get help because we don't deal with
documents over 50, 60 years old.

GT: 00:32:33 That's crazy. So, he was able to fool the FBI as well.

George: 00:32:40 Oh, yeah. On the one document, *The Oath of a Freeman*, which he was trying to sell for one and a half million dollars at the time the bombings occurred. The document had been authenticated by the FBI, the American Antiquarian Society, the Library of Congress, an independent laboratory in Dallas and also in Kansas City.

GT: 00:32:57 That's like six different organizations. Right? So, he was able to fool six organizations with a toy store chemistry set.

George: 00:33:03 In fact, the funny thing in my career there, the New York Times wrote an article. He said, "Everybody says it's genuine except some two-bit hick in Utah."

George: 00:33:15 So I had that moniker placed on my desk. {chuckles} But ultimately, we were proven to be right because in fact all of the books that were written back and were wrong. We had to do the proper examination research and so forth to find out why. One of the things is the book said that ink will crack as it grows older. That is not absolutely correct and that's one of the problems with science. We have some egotistical scientists in this world, believe it or not, that say "My way is the only way." There's always another way to do something it seems like. They may be right many times, but there's a way of fooling them and that's what Mark Hofmann did.

GT:		<u>00:34:00</u>	Wow.

More Hofmann Techniques & Forged Sports Memorabilia

Introduction

We're continuing our conversation with George Throckmorton. In this next episode, George describes aging techniques that Mark Hofmann used to make his forgeries appear older than they were. We'll also discuss sports memorabilia. George tells that the majority of those "Authentic" jerseys, balls, and bats are forged. How does he know? Check out our conversation.

GT:	00:34:00	So, let's talk about that. With the aging process, how were you able to duplicate? Because I think this cracking ink was a big piece that you figured out. That's how it was a forgery, right?
George:	00:34:10	That was really the first time we realized something was wrong. The church let us have a room down in their library and we got a special lock put on it just to make sure they wouldn't come in an after-hours. I mean, I shouldn't say we didn't trust him, but we didn't. All of the rumors going there about how they're hiding things and trying to hide things and I would walk in and people would--in fact later on, the director of the library down there as I went in and he would say, "George, you realize that people here don't like you, don't you?"
George:	00:34:10	I said, "I know that."

George: 00:34:45   He says, "That's okay. You still can have anything you want."

George: 00:34:47   Because they didn't like to see me come in. They have accepted these as documents. I had a very high person. Like I say he's published many books. He's not alive anymore. I'm not going to use his name, but when I called him to talk to him on the phone, he started hollering at me over the phone telling me I don't know what I'm doing and I'm trying to blackmail somebody, Mark Hofmann. Mark Hofmann's honest and all this other stuff, and I finally hung up on him. I got tired of hearing him holler at me. But historians are the same way. They examined a document. They determined it's genuine, but from their own perspective, not from a scientific analysis. And although the church tried, and they did, President Hinckley had a document he personally paid to get authenticated and he sent it. Who is the best document examiner?

George: 00:35:40   Well, there's two people back east, one in Boston, one in New York, and they sent them back and they got them authenticated. Who are they going to believe? I mean, they've been known. The one fellow back in New York had published 12 different books, I think it was, on how to detect a forged historical document. He's considered by himself if nobody else to be the greatest document examiner in the world and had for years. He was 80 when I met him. Wonderful man. He really is. But he didn't know the first thing about a chemical analysis and the significance of it. And so, the church tried the best they could to find people they thought could authenticate documents and they got them authenticated. It's just they weren't using the right techniques. And they didn't know because we're a document examiner, forensic document examiners, we don't deal with historical documents. But when we had to, we started applying the scientific methods and we found out that their methods were all wrong.

GT: 00:36:36   So, you know, this brings up a point, there's a TV show. I know my dad loves to watch it called *Pawn Stars* and you know, they'll bring a lot of people will bring in stuff into the pawn shop and then they will bring in a historical expert and say, "Is this legitimate?" Are those sorts of things legitimate analyses?

George: 00:36:54   Over the years, they had that come to Salt Lake a few years ago. I don't know if you're aware of that. And the person that they brought into authenticate documents, owned a bookstore downtown. That was their expert. I've also, over the years, I've done a lot of work on sports memorabilia. I had a Babe Ruth jersey that was selling for $750,000.

GT: 00:37:19   Oh my goodness.

George: 00:37:22   It had been authenticated. But it wasn't [genuine.] Because the ink that was used to sign it wasn't made until--Babe Ruth died in 1948. And Ink wasn't made until 1972, so if it had been genuine, he would've had to been resurrected and signed his name. {chuckles} But I met with a

lot of these people that had authenticated it and I
found out they count a baseball, for instance, has
to have mud on it. I didn't know that. Any major
league baseball, they rub it in the mud from
Cooperstown or wherever it is, where baseball
was invented.

George: 00:37:49   That's still a tradition. So, they look for residue of
the mud. They count the number of stitches in
the ball because they change the stitches
periodically as they manufactured for that
particular year. And that's how they're doing it.
Well, I don't know anything about that. That's not
my expertise.

George: 00:38:07   Historians, when they look at documents, they
look at the content of it. What does it say? What
else was going on historically at that particular
point? That's how they authenticate it. When I
testified about the *Salamander Letter* in court, I
had never read the contents of it. I didn't know
what it said other than what people had told me.
In fact, to this day, I don't know whether I read it.
I think I did, just out of curiosity, but we don't
look at what the words are. We look at the ink,
the strokes, the paper, things like that, the
absorption rate. And so, everybody has their own
expertise and the only way you can really get it
accurate as if you have all these various branches
of science go in and look at it. That's too
expensive to do if your document is only going to
be $100 and you're going to spend $5,000 to get
it authenticated. By the way, the fellow that
authenticated the *Salamander Letter*, his fee was
$6,000 to authenticate it. Outrageous in my

humble opinion, but he did things I never knew
of.

GT: <u>00:38:07</u>   Oh Wow.

George: <u>00:39:10</u>   I'm sorry. Did that answer your question?

GT: <u>00:39:18</u>   So yeah. But anyway, for shows like that, they're
                                probably not really good analysis? Is that
                                [correct?]

George: <u>00:39:21</u>   Not really. And the sports show, sports
                                memorabilia, they use a different thing than we
                                do. They tried hiring a document examiner. Some
                                of these sports shows did. Ted Williams, for
                                instance, would make $100,000 a day, which was
                                more than he earned in a year while he was
                                working, to go down and sign autographs and
                                they tried to hire one of our people to go down
                                there and give certificates of authentication. They
                                couldn't find them, because we have to provide a
                                thorough examination. So every signature is going
                                to take one to two hours to do an examination.
                                And you know, how many hundreds or thousands
                                of these certificates are issued today? So, we told
                                them we wouldn't do it, so they went out and
                                hired one of the others that is not trained
                                properly but still claims to be a document
                                examiner and they don't know the difference. So,
                                there's a lot of that that goes on.

GT: <u>00:40:19</u>   Wow. So, I mean, can we have a lot of faith in any
                                of these historical documents?

George: 00:40:25   Years ago I was interviewed in *60 Minutes* back in New York. They called me back to look at some sports memorabilia and I thought it was kind of funny and I didn't know it was as significant as they did, but they always had a part where you would have one final statement before they ended the program and they said, "What's your advice to people that goes out and buys sports memorabilia?"

George: 00:40:52   And I made the comment, I says, "I would suggest that they pay as little as possible because it's probably forged, anyway." That's how they ended the program. And the *New York Times* did an article that says about 7 out of 10 sports things are forged.

GT: 00:40:52   Really?

George: 00:41:06   And I did some work for the FBI years ago in Cincinnati where they broke into a guy's house and he found he had in his garage. He was forging sports memorabilia on anything: baseballs, bats, uniforms, cards. He had a machine that did it. It is called an autopen. And so, I wouldn't be surprised if 7 out of 10 are forged.

GT: 00:41:06   Really? It's that high.

George: 00:41:32   I don't know how much it is in historical documents.

GT: 00:41:32   In sports memorabilia, it's probably that.

George: 00:41:38   That was the estimate they gave. I don't doubt it.

George: 00:41:38   Wow, that's crazy.

George: 00:41:42   In fact, that's one of the reasons I worked for an auction house out of California and they didn't like me after a while because everything they would send me was forged.

George: 00:41:51   Really? Every single document they sent me it was forged.

GT: 00:41:51   Oh my goodness.

George: 00:41:55   Well that's not good. You can't sell it. When you want to sell that Babe Ruth Jersey for $750,000 and it's forged. They lost a lot of money on that transaction because you know, they get a percentage of that when they try to sell it.

GT: 00:42:11   Well I understand that there's a market for some of Mark Hofmann's forgeries now.

George: 00:42:13   Oh sure. But not a million and a half dollars.

GT: 00:42:13   Right.

George: 00:42:20   I think the *Salamander Letter* sold for, I think it was either 40 to 60, somewhere in that and I don't know where it is now. I don't know who owns it, but I know it's not worth that much.

George: 00:42:31   Wow. So, was it you or was it Bill that, that came up with this? I think it was ammonia residue or something?

George: 00:42:35   I'm sorry, I got sidetracked. I get sidetracked so much. You asked me how we detect it? We got this room, the church let us have a room, and as I said, we put a lock on it and every night, or every morning they would bring us the documents. I put them in my briefcase. I locked the briefcase with the documents they brought me. At night I would take it up and put it back in their safe and I would handcuff it to one of the pipes, so they couldn't get to it. I mean, that's the trust we had back then.

GT: 00:42:35   Wow.

George: 00:43:08   And as we was looking at the documents for anything, we didn't know what to look for. We did look at historical documents and Bill would look at some, and I will look at some, and we had a microscope. We had an ultraviolet light. And I started noticing some things.

George: 00:43:24   I don't know what Bill was looking at it quite frankly. But we were, you know, two, three feet apart is all. We were in the same room which was locked, and nobody had access to that. We had a special lock put on. We was the only one that had a key. And we spent two weeks in that room, Bill and I did. And in the process of that we're looking at documents and requesting more and then we would ask the head of the library there, the significance, the history and so forth. And there was one document I was looking at, and I noticed. I call it my Rosetta Stone because it was a document which was historical document on purchasing some land which later became Nauvoo. And I noticed that there was different things on that one document. There was different inks, different pens.

George: <u>00:44:15</u> And as I put an ultraviolet light, there was some part that would reflect back and other parts that would not. And that really caused me some question. Why? If this document has been saved for over 100 years, why would you have some part that glowed and some part that did not, different inks, and so forth? And as I looked at it closer, I noticed the thing that made the document valuable was not the date itself, but the fact that it says, "obliged Joseph Smith." And where it said, "obliged Joseph Smith" was where I saw different ink and I saw this white effect going around and I asked him that night, I asked him, I says, "Can you tell us where this came from?" Because before we started noticing some of these documents that have blue haze on the documents under ultraviolet light. Others did not.

George: <u>00:45:02</u> And so we separated them into two piles. And as I looked at those under the microscope, I noticed there was a characteristic of the ink would crack on some of them, not others. And then I noticed the ones with that blue haze, we're also the ones that had that had the blue there, the cracked ink. And so, I told Bill, I said, "Bill," I says, "I think we got something here." And I handed him a stack of documents and I says, "You give them to me, mix them up, give them to me and I'll tell you which one came through the hands of Hofmann." And he gave it to me and I looked under the microscope and he says, "this one did." He gave me another one. "This one did not," and so forth

until we were through. And all of them that had
the cracked ink had Hofmann's signature, or had
Hofmann.

George: 00:45:52 He had either donated it or sold it to the church
or something. The others had not come through
Hofmann except for one document. And that was
the one I mentioned where there were two
different types of inks and so forth. And so that
night as we was getting ready to leave. I asked the
librarian there. I says, "Could you tell me? Did this
come through the hands of Hofmann?"

George: 00:45:52 And he said, "No."

George: 00:46:14 Well that shot our whole theory. And so, we went
home, and I was very discouraged. The next
morning, we were up there, and he took me up
and brought me back from the safe and he said,
"Oh, by the way, that document you gave me.
That did come through the hands of Hofmann"

George: 00:46:32 We thought, "We've got it!" And then that was
our first clue, the blue hazing and the cracked ink,
and this one that had both on them. That was our
Rosetta Stone. All of these Hofmann handled.
These, he did not. And from there on, then we
started doing experimentation. What caused the
ink? That is what Bill took. What caused the blue
ink there? That blue hazing, that's what I took.
And so, it's a matter of research, study, and
experimentation.

GT: 00:46:59 So how long after the bombs? The bombs were
October of '85, right?

George: 00:46:59   Correct.

GT: 00:47:04   How long until you discovered this blue hazing
                       and cracked ink?

George: 00:47:09   That was about March. So that still wasn't
                       sufficient because we continued researching until
                       May, before we really started catching on. Even
                       then we didn't find the chemicals, for instance,
                       from the toy store. We didn't find that for five
                       more months.

GT: 00:47:09   Wow.

George: 00:47:27   This investigation took us 16 months full-time.
                       That's how long I was involved in it.

GT: 00:47:27   Wow, so how long before Hofmann went to trial
                       then?

George: 00:47:34   Again, the bombs occurred. He wasn't arrested
                       until, I think January because he was still
                       recovering. The district attorney had somebody
                       watching him all the time. They had a car up at his
                       house watching and so forth. And the preliminary
                       hearing, to me that's just the lesser trial. There's
                       no jury, but it's a trial. It's a full-fledged trial
                       except the judge presides and determines
                       whether it should go before a jury or not. The
                       preliminary hearing lasted either four or five
                       weeks and that started in May. I know that
                       because there was nothing I could do. They
                       wouldn't let him in the courtroom. And so, I took
                       my family and we flew back to Florida and went

to Disney World back there for a week. We got some good cheap fares.

GT: 00:47:34   Oh good.

George: 00:48:18   So I was gone for a week during that period of time. But, I testified, and Bill came up and testified, I think about the third week.

GT: 00:48:29   So yeah, there was a preliminary hearing, so that was in January?

George: 00:48:29   May.

GT: 00:48:35   May of '86. So that's one of the preliminary hearing was. I know we talked on the phone a little bit about the FBI. Can you talk a little bit about your interactions with them?

George: 00:48:49   Yeah, I'm retired now, so I can. The FBI had authenticated several of these documents and anybody in law enforcement knows you don't mess with the FBI. And we, Bill Flynn actually knew the examiner at the FBI that examined the *Salamander Letter*. When I started in the investigation I had to visit several of the laboratories. For instance, I visited the Secret Service Laboratory and the FBI laboratory, and the New York State Crime Laboratory up there to visit with people and look at some of the documents that they had that we did not have access to.

George: 00:49:36   And I can give you an example. When I was working at the Institute of Applied Science in

Chicago in 1970, I met a man by the name of Tony Cantu. He worked for the secret service. Him and two other people were responsible for doing all of the publications, research and so forth on ink. This is the three greatest ink experts in the world. Tony and I became friends and that's good, because when I had to go back to New York for instance, and look at the *Oath of a Freeman*, the original, they wouldn't let us see it out. They wouldn't send it out there because it was worth too much money. They didn't want to let it go. So, I tried. I actually called one of the people at the lab and he kept hanging up on me. As soon as he found out it was me, he would hang up.

George: 00:50:28   And so, I hadn't contacted Tony yet. I was talking to another fellow that Tony worked with on college research. Anyway, so I got the attorney general to contact the attorney general of New York and he authorized me to go back and look into the state laboratory, so I could look at this document. Again, it's a million bucks. They don't want to let it go. So, I flew back there, and I went in the lab right after lunch. And the fellow that had the document and so forth was the director of the lab. He wasn't in at the time he was out to lunch, so I was sitting there and as he walked in the door, I stood up, the secretary said, "Oh, Mr. so and so, this is Mr. Throckmorton." And he had his hand out towards me and then as soon as he heard the name, he pulled it back. He turned around and went in and slammed the door in the back of me. Somebody else had to bring the document because they had already authenticated it, and no, this two-bit hick from

Utah was not going to come out and contradict him.

George: 00:51:23   I went down to Washington, D.C. to look at some of them and I met Tony and he was with me all day long. We went around and I'm glad he was. We would go into the FBI lab as soon as they walked in. "Hi Tony. How you doing? It's good to see you. Hi, this is George." And they would all turn around and walk away. Secret Service lab was the same thing. When we called for help, they wouldn't talk to us because we're contradicting what the FBI had said, and other laboratories too. And that lasted actually until 1987 in October, so we were black-balled for over a year and a half and finally we met in Palm Springs, California. We met for three days to discuss how Hofmann did his forgery with the forensic examiners from around the country and we wanted to be FBI to come because everybody knew they made a mistake.

George: 00:52:19   Hofmann had already confessed and we had met our own regional organizations and we'd put on programs there. Everybody knew the FBI made a mistake. So, we wanted them to come out and tell us what happened because they don't make mistakes. They really don't. In this case, they did. And so, they finally agreed to come down to Palm Springs where we had our meeting. The meeting we had in the Gene Autry Hotel down there was good because there were three FBI agents meeting with me in the room and I told them, "We don't want to embarrass you, but we need to let the other examiners know what went wrong so they don't make mistakes."

George: 00:52:56   We would discuss a plan and one agent went in the other room, called Washington, come back and said, "Nope, we can't use that approach." We tried another one.

George: 00:53:03   He went back and finally on the third one, he came back and said, "Okay. That's the approach. We're going to make our presentation." And from then on, they had some ill feelings towards us, but they at least cooperated.

George: 00:53:16   Wow. That must've been pretty interesting to take on the FBI.

George: 00:53:20   It was a very traumatic period of time. I couldn't talk to my wife about these things, and that was frustration. Everybody said we were wrong. Everybody said we were wrong, but Bill and I thank goodness for Bill. I would have caved in. I would have said, I don't care, and quit. I think I probably would have, but because of the support I had from him and we knew we were right, just how are we going to convince them? That's why it took so long in the *Salamander Letter*. It wasn't enough just to come up with a couple of things.

George: 00:53:50   There were actually seven different things that combined together refuted what the FBI said. For instance, the paper. It was genuine paper. He stole it out of a book up at the University of Utah. He stole that one, the back or front fly leaves, I don't know. But they couldn't trace it back to the book. He went through and he drew lines on the paper.

GT: 00:53:50   Oh, Wow.

George: 00:54:16   So it was lined paper and so the FBI would look at it, "Oh, this is lined. This is not. Let it go." Remember the postmark? The FBI saw the postmark, but they never looked at it to see if it was real or not. They just saw the postmark. They'd said that saw it cost six cents to be mailed. It was addressed to the right person. It was folded properly. It was sealed with sealing wax. The paper was genuine, so they thought it was genuine.

George: 00:54:43   When we found out the sealing wax was counterfeited, it was a combination of things. We found out that the paper was actually lined with pencil and as I was measuring the lines, they were not parallel. They were close. He used a ruler. I used a ruler that's good within 1/125th of an inch, under the microscope. And I found out they weren't parallel. They had to be parallel if they were printed, but the FBI never looked at that. So those are the things that we looked at. And finally, between the seven of them, we found it was enough that the FBI finally consented. Reluctantly, but they consented. It was forged.

GT: 00:55:24   Wow. That's crazy. That's awesome.

Who was the 3rd Bomb Intended for?

Introduction

Mark Hofmann's first two bombs killed Steve Christensen and Kathy Sheets. In this next episode, we will talk about the third bomb. Who was it likely intended for? Was it a suicide attempt as some people believe, or was it intended for someone else? George gives some important details on the crime scene. Check out our conversation…

GT: 00:55:24   Let's talk a little bit about the bomb that actually injured Hofmann. I know there were some things in the trunk of the car. I was just reading the book Salamander yesterday, trying to refresh my memory on some of these things. Why were police initially suspecting that Hofmann blew up himself essentially?

George: 00:55:58   Originally, they suspected Hofmann was doing something wrong because he was not telling the story that was consistent with the evidence. He mentioned that he had gone back to his car and as he opened the door, the bomb fell out of the car and blew him up. The bomb that blew up Hofmann, we already had a representative from [Bureau of] Alcohol, Tobacco, and Firearms, ATF. They were out here because of the two bombs that had happened previous to this one. And so, they were in town when this third bomb went off. And so, they were at the scene and these are the experts. Those are the experts on bombs. And they were examining the scene. And then when the investigator said that Hofmann had told him the bomb fell out of the car, he said, "That's not true. He's not telling you the truth."

George: 00:56:54   Well, when somebody is not telling you the truth, you wonder why. In looking in the trunk, they found some old documents that didn't matter. He was legitimate examiner. Everybody knew that, but they also found some components of a pipe bomb in the trunk.

GT: 00:56:54   Oh, I didn't know that.

George: 00:57:15   Later on the investigation revealed that Hofmann had made the pipe bombs and all of the previous, the previous two, and this one, was all made basically the same way. The switches that were used were purchased at Radio Shack. As the investigation continued, the investigators found where he had purchased these fuses, switches for the pipe bombs, and he really tried to hide it. I believe, and I can't remember for sure, it's been a long time, but this was what was reported to me by the investigators that one of the switches was found at a Radio Shack in Wyoming. Another one was found at the Radio Shack in Colorado. He never bought them all at the same time. He spread himself out and he used a different name. Back then when you bought something at Radio Shack, they always asked your name. He put down the name of Mike Hansen. Ironically, in a shop in Colorado where he purchased something. I can't remember what it was. He was by Mike Hansen and he wrote out a check to them, but on the check of Mike Hansen was found the fingerprint of Mark Hofmann. We thought we were looking for two different people at first.

GT: 00:58:37   Oh Wow. Yeah.

George: 00:58:38   We found this is the same person, and again, this is an instance where the investigators never thought to process the check for fingerprints and having worked fingerprints in to state lab, I said "Send it out to the state lab and asked them to process it for fingerprints." And they did, and they found the one fingerprint of Mark Hofmann on the check for Mike Hansen, so they knew it was the same person. And then as they went around, they found these switches had been purchased by Mike Hansen, so in effect they were actually purchased by Mark Hofmann. So, all of the bombs were made by the same person.

George: 00:59:15   Why were some of these bomb parts found in the trunk of the car? Why was Mark Hofmann lying? Later on, when they suspected that they do a much more thorough investigation and they found out there was a mercury switch, which simply means they used to use them a lot in light switches. They have two wires that are at the top and they have mercury at the bottom and when you turn it, the mercury will flow down, make a connection, and that's why it's called a mercury switch. So long as you carry it upright, you can carry it around. They found Mark Hofmann was waiting to see somebody at the Crossroads Mall downtown and at the time he would meet this person on a specific day at a specific time. Hofmann made this third bomb. He went down to

Crossroads Mall. He parked his car up where the Conference Center is presently at. It was across the street from the old Deseret Gym.

George: 01:00:19   And he carried the bomb with him down to the mall. We know he was there for at least an hour and a half carrying the bomb because he had gone into a local store and made a purchase there. And it had the time on the receipt. It was in his pocket. So, we know he was there. And then I think what happened, and we have to speculate, but it seems pretty good. When this person didn't show up, then Hofmann left. He walked back up to his car, which was a low sportscar. As he opened up the car door, he was still carrying the bomb. As he sits down in the seat and goes to put the bomb on the passenger seat. It hit the gearshift knob and caused it to tip and it blew him out of the car. That was totally contrary to what he said happened.

George: 01:01:12   So we know he was lying. And you start putting two and two together and it comes up with some assumptions there. If he had got into the car and shut the door, he would have been blown to bits. Literally he had been blown to several pieces, but because the door was open, it blew off part of his kneecap and one of his fingers and that means he was holding the bomb and because it blew off part of his kneecap, that's where the explosion came after hitting the gear shift knob on the floor.

George: 01:01:42   Now a side note on that if you want, there were two construction workers who was having lunch, at least two that were having lunch on the wall when the bomb went off. They ran down, and they noticed that Hofmann had temple garments on and the one pulled out some oil, which he carried. It's a good thing about Mormon sometimes. They can carry interesting things in their pockets. But anyway, and they blessed him and commanded him to live and he did. I've often wondered. Scientifically, he lived because the door was not shut. Religiously speaking. He lives maybe because the door was not shut, and they gave him a blessing. If he would have died, the case would have been closed within 12 hours because they had enough evidence to indicate he made the bombs and that's all that matters. You don't need a motive if somebody is dead. But because he lived, they needed to have a motive. Why? And that's what took the investigation so long.

GT: 01:02:41   So I've heard there's speculation. I actually talked with Shannon Flynn[2] who was a good friend with Mark Hofmann and he believes that this was a really a suicide attempt.[3] I've heard other people speculate that it might've been for Lynn Jacobs or Brent Ashworth or Metcalfe?

George: 01:02:41   Brent Metcalfe.

GT: 01:03:03   Yeah, Brent Metcalfe. And so, do you have any ideas who that third bomb was intended for?

---

[2] See interview at https://wp.me/p8l6gx-j6
[3] See interview at https://gospeltangents.com/2017/10/15/would-mark-hofmann-kill-again/

George: 01:03:06   Oh yeah. It's commonly known as Brent
Ashworth.

GT: 01:03:08   It was that to Brent Ashworth.

George: 01:03:13   He know that too, Brent does. I wouldn't say it.
Excuse me. He goes out and talks about it. I have
been around him many times in the last several
years and the facts of the investigation [lead us to
believe] it was him. He was the one that he was
due to meet at the Crossroads Mall. See, Brent is
an attorney and he had some affiliates up in
Crossroads Mall and every, I think it was every
Wednesday he would come down and meet with
them and he would go up to the 17th floor and
meet with them. So, if Mark ever wanted to meet
with him. He would meet him by the escalator
coming up toward where the elevators were. And
so, he was there waiting for him. And Brent
coincidentally again, happened to come up the
day before for some unknown reason. Mark
actually visited him on Sunday before the bombs
to make sure he was coming down there.

GT: 01:03:56   Oh really?

George: 01:04:02   And so Mark was waiting for him and Brent
showed up the day before. I'm reminded of the
story of the three little pigs and the wolf. But
anyway, and then he waited until he had a chance
to come down and when Brent didn't come down,
that's when he left and went back to his car. So, it
was Brent.

GT: 01:04:02   It was Brent, wow.

George: 01:04:19   And think of the cold-blooded nature to give him a bomb as he gets in the elevator.

GT: 01:04:24   Oh Wow. That's terrible. So, let's talk a little bit about what was in the trunk. I remember reading in the book *Salamander*, I believe they said that you were upset because, you know, with the big fire and everything, the fire department obviously came and got a lot of the documents wet and then they were laid out to dry, not very, hygienically I guess. Could you talk a little bit about what was in that trunk?

George: 01:04:59   Well, I can tell you what I saw, cause again, I wasn't involved for another six weeks. But when I finally got involved in it, I went down to the police department and they took me down, that was the old police department before they built the new building. It's where the library is now downtown Salt Lake and down in the basement they had a gymnasium where they would play basketball. And as they walked down in the basement, spread out all over the basketball floor was these documents drying out and then there was another room to the side which they kept locked where they had file cabinets and other boxes of documents that they had taken from Hofmann. But they were all still spread out, drying out.

George: 01:05:47   I mean this is six weeks later and they had not been inventoried. I don't know whether they ever were inventoried. I don't know. Again, I was with the Attorney General's office. I didn't care what the police department did. All I cared is they weren't maintained properly, and I never got a chance to see everything there. They just said, "Well, here they are, look around and see what you might want," and I would go in the room, for instance, and went through the file cabinet and looked at various things that were never introduced in evidence. For instance, I found some letters from Heber J. Grant. There was a whole stack of them, maybe 20-30 of them. Of course, Heber J. Grant was one of the presidents of the church. And it said, "Dear brother, so-and-so." That was left blank.

George: 01:06:37   It said, "I want to thank you for allowing me to stay at your house when I visited conference." And again, we're speculating, why did he have so many? Because he was probably going around to relatives and saying, here's a letter I found. Would you like to buy it for 100 bucks?" Or something like that. And we don't know how many he used. We never did the investigation again. There were a total of 12 or 13 of us working full time for 16 months. We had to focus our attention on the documents that costs one and a half million dollars rather than the ones he may sell for 50 bucks. And if you remember when they went to trial or when he was arrested, he was arrested for I think two counts of homicide, 28 counts of fraud or something. And that was modified significantly too. Yeah.

GT: 01:06:37   Hmm.

George: 01:07:32   Does that answer your question?

GT: 01:07:35   Yeah.

Why Hofmann Killed his Best Friends

Introduction

Mark Hofmann was a successful document dealer in the 1980s. Why did he kill? Document Examiner George Throckmorton gives his insights into the Hofmann case. Check out our conversation....

GT: 01:07:35   So why do you think Mark killed? I believe when we were talking on the phone. It seems like you said that Mark said that Steve Christensen was his best friend, and that he killed his best friend. Why do you think that was?

George: 01:07:56   Yes. I'll explain it. Now realize if you talk to various investigators, they have their own theory and they do. Each investigator kind of has their theory. My particular theory along with one of the attorneys came to being because of the investigation we did. They couldn't convince us of their theory. It didn't hold water and a couple of others have bought on to this too. But our seems most logical and it involved not only the examination of the documents, but I went out with this other attorney two or three times to question other people and then I just started putting the pieces of the puzzle together.

George: 01:08:44   Ours forms the most perfect picture in my opinion. And here's the way it went. First of all, the *Oath of a Freeman*. The *Oath of a Freeman* is supposed to be the first printed document in the colonies. The

Massachusetts Bay Colony wanted to get a printing press here. So, they ordered one from England to come over on the boat. While it was coming over, they met together in the city council and they said, what should be the first document to come off the printing press when it gets here? And this was discussed. Historically, these are the records we have and there's four different versions of what the Oath said. But they all basically said the same thing: in order to be a free man, and of course this is the land of the free, and this is why it's so significant. You had to belong to a church, you had to be married, you had to own a house.

George: <u>01:09:42</u> If you can do that, you were then allowed to vote. And so, if you met those qualifications, you could go down and, and be sworn in or take the oath of a freeman and that would allow you the opportunity to vote. Hofmann, we know, heard that a firm by the name of Schiller & Wapner in New York was looking for the *Oath*. They had advertised in magazines. And this is what we believe happened. Mark Hofmann flew back to New York and researched it. What should be the contents? And he took these four versions and made his own. And then he came back to Salt Lake. And he did, we call it a cut and paste. He'd made Xerox copies of this type style that was used to print documents back then. And it was different than it is today. And, he made it say the words he wanted to say.

George: <u>01:10:43</u> He took a picture of it and then he had a plate made, a printing plate. And so, he had what he was going to consider was the *Oath of a Freeman*, but because it would be so valuable, he made another document and he called it the *Oath of a Freeman* and it was a poem. We don't know what it really was, but it said *Oath of a*

Freeman. He took this *Oath of a Freeman* back to New York, went in a bookstore, an old bookstore, went in the back, wasted about an hour looking through things came up and he made purchases of four or five documents and he made certain that the cash register wrote on the receipt, what the name of these documents were. This is not normal, but he made sure he did it and one of them was the *Oath of a Freeman*. He then flew back to Salt Lake. He got off the plane, he come back and he took this *Oath* that he actually smuggled into the store and then bought. He brought it back. He left it here. He got the *Oath* that he had prepared. He now flies back to New York and he goes to Schiller and Wapner's. He pretends. He's an excellent white-collar criminal. He pretends to be stupid. He pretends to be the hick from Utah and I've said it many times, and this is my own feelings. I says I wouldn't be surprised if he had some cow manure on the bottom of his shoes just to convince him how stupid he was, but he walks in and he says, "I bought this document over at this bookstore over here," and he holds it up and it pretends to have no idea what it is. And as they looked at it, they immediately knew what it was because they've been advertising, looking for it. And so, he pretends to be stupid and dumb and all this other stuff.

George: <u>01:12:19</u> How dumb he was. He walked out of that store with a $60,000 check in his pocket. That $60,000 check gave Schiller and Wapner the right to sell his document for over a million dollars. If they sold at less than a million dollars, he would get all of the proceeds in order for them to make anything, they had to sell it for more than a million dollars. They gave him $60,000 for that right. So, he walks out with $60,000. They have that, and they're assured they can sell it for one and a half million dollars. It would be the first document in the colonies, especially showing that it's freedom. They expected it to be on display next to the Declaration of Independence. So, he gets back, and he starts a big spending spree. He's got a lot of money now. He gets him a new house. He gets him a new car.

George: 01:13:14 He pays cash for his car and a bunch of other stuff. He knows he's getting this million bucks back here, at least $500,000 because they won't sell it unless he's getting $500,000. So anyway. And then he thought, boy, that's good. So now he decides I'm going to do it again. So, he makes a second *Oath of a Freeman*. He actually made a third, which he was trying to sell down in Brazil, but I don't know how many people knew that. The second one he sells to somebody up in Idaho and I'm not going to describe him. I know it'd be interesting, but if I describe him, there might be a lot of people that know who it is. But there's a fellow up in Idaho and he sells it to him for $100,000. And as time progresses, the *Oath* back in New York isn't selling as quickly as they thought.

George: 01:14:02 The American Antiquarian Society, the Library of Congress, they wanted it, but they didn't want to pay over a million dollars. They were only going to pay $750,000 for it. They had it authenticated as far as they could and so forth and etc. So, the sale is being delayed quite a bit, several months. But he still knows it's coming in. So that's why he sells us one. He gets $100,000 and then later on the person up in Idaho, he sees where they got the *Oath of a Freeman* back in New York. And they're selling it and he says, "This isn't an original that I purchased. Hofmann told me it was an original." So, he called him on the phone, and he says, "So is this isn't an original." He actually meets with him and says, "This is not an original document, is not worth $100,000. I want my money back." Mark doesn't have any money. And apparently an argument ensued or something.

George: <u>01:14:59</u> And Mark gets physically assaulted. This was the first time in his life, we know of, that somebody actually physically assaulted him. Before he's dealing with, what do they call him, Mr. Milk Toasts. You know, historians are generally laid back, calm person. I don't know anybody other than a couple that hollered at me. But most of them I don't think they do. And nobody had ever hit him before. He had bounced checks on him. He would lie to them about documents and that. And it was well known. He was like that. But they wanted to go back to him because he could provide the documents they wanted. He took orders for documents frequently and miraculously found them. But anyway, this guy up in Idaho, he beat him up. Hofmann didn't know what to think. Nobody's ever hit him before and he's a coward. That's why they bomb. Because you don't have to be there when somebody gets injured. And, so anyway, the guy says, "I want my money back and I want it next Monday," or whatever it was. Now what is he going to do? Now this is speculative, but it seems to make sense from the bits of pieces of puzzle that we put together.

George: <u>01:16:12</u> He says, "What can I do so he won't come after me and hit me anymore?" And he's thinking, you know, "If one of my best friends die, I'll have an excuse to go to his funeral and he won't come back. He'll give me a few days. By then the *Oath* will be sold back there."

And in fact, I think it was the American Antiquarian Society was meeting to discuss purchasing it again on Tuesday or Wednesday of that week. We know that because we saw the agenda for the meeting. And again, I don't know how many of the other investigators saw this, but we did. That's why this is another piece that we had that others did not, so that day of either Tuesday or Wednesday is crucial because that's when they're voting to buy it. And Schiller & Wapner convinced him they're going to buy it, so he knows he's going to get it. So, he needs to postpone just a couple of days before this guy comes back and beats him up again. And so, we found in his possession a three by five card that had five of his closest friends written, their names written on it in Mark's handwriting. And by the name of Steve Christensen was an asterisk. We're assuming that he put the asterisk there. But anyway, so it was one of his five closest friends he had to kill so he could go to their funeral. The bombs came up. Steve Christensen was blown up and of course the second bomb was a diversionary thing for the police department, which they believed for several days that they were involved, not in the *Salamander Letter*, but involved in financial dealings down in Las Vegas.

George: <u>01:17:53</u> The irony of that is the news media didn't believe that. They kept putting *Salamander Letter*. So, what is Hofmann hearing about that the police are investigating Las Vegas or are they investigating the *Salamander Letter*? All he sees is the *Salamander Letter*. So, he's a little concerned more and then he gets a call from the guy and he says, "Hey, you got to wait for a couple of days. My best friend got killed and going to his funeral."

George: <u>01:18:15</u> He says, "I don't care. I want my money back. And if you're not around and coming after your family."

George: <u>01:18:23</u> Good old farmer, I love farmers. I am an old farmer as a kid. But anyway, so now the next phase is what can I do so we won't come after me and my family? And he thought, "You know, if there's another bomb related to *Salamander* or historical documents, that'll give me an excuse to say they're coming after me." And that's what he told his friends and his friends were concerned about him too. And he lied to each one of the friends. If the friends could ever get together and hear what he had told everybody, and if you remind me about the hot tub, I'll tell you about that.

GT: <u>01:18:23</u> Oh, yeah. We'll talk about that.

George: <u>01:19:03</u> But anyway, so that's where he goes after Brent Ashworth, who's a well-known collector of historical documents and if a Brent gets blown up, then he'll have an excuse to leave town, Hofmann will. And that's why he was going after Brent. But then he accidentally blew up himself.

GT: <u>01:19:22</u> Didn't he have a good enough excuse? Because I talked with Curt Bench and Curt said the first person he called after Steve Christensen was killed was Mark Hofmann.[4] And [Curt] said, "Mark, you've got to be careful. There's a bomber out there," which is just so crazy to me.

George: <u>01:19:42</u> See, I don't know whether Mark got the excuse because of people telling him, "You've got to be

---

[4] See https://gospeltangents.com/2017/05/25/bomb-day-1-2-killed-october-15-1985/

careful," or what. And of course, Brent Ashworth left town too, if you're familiar with that.

GT: 01:19:42 Yeah.

George: 01:19:55 Which was a sad experience. But all of these people involved were leaving town. So, if Mark left, that's nothing unusual.

GT: 01:20:03 Well, and Curt said the next day when the third bomb went off, that I think he said he was driving to work and he heard the news, or maybe it was a lunch break, I think it was. And he said he punched the steering wheel and said, "Mark, you weren't careful. You weren't careful."

George: 01:20:23 Well, he wasn't. Unfortunately, he blew themselves up instead of somebody else blowing him up. But the rumors were running so rampant at that time and so it would be natural for Mark to leave town and hide. Others were doing it too. And so that way this guy from Idaho couldn't begrudge him. Everybody's leaving.

GT: 01:20:40 Well, yeah, I mean it would make sense to me. I'm not a criminal so maybe I don't think like a criminal, but if Brent Ashworth is leaving town and you know, Curt's looking for bombs in his house, and Shannon is checking his car for bombs and you know, everybody was really concerned about this, why wouldn't [Mark]?

GT: 01:21:03 And, if Mark is concerned about this farmer from Idaho, why not just leave town unannounced? I mean that would make sense to me, but.

George: <u>01:21:12</u> Oh, you want him to know that you're gone and that's why this guy is not coming down, beating up your family or whatever.

GT   <u>01:21:12</u> Well, because...

George: <u>01:21:12</u> I'm hiding.

GT: <u>01:21:12</u> Yeah.

George: <u>01:21:23</u> I believe, and it is just my theory. I believe he have called the guy up and says, "Hey, there's bombs going off. Many of us are leaving town so I won't be able to get to you for at least a couple of days until things quiet down." That's my feeling.

GT: <u>01:21:36</u> Well, and the other thing, it sounds like Mark was trying to make this a diversionary tactic. He killed Steve Christensen and then I believe the second bomb was intended for Gary Sheets. But his wife picked it up and it killed her.

George: <u>01:21:54</u> Realize, it didn't matter. It was laying on the floor, on the ground out by the car. So, if anybody, even if it didn't go off, if they found the bomb there, it would've connected the two together.

GT: <u>01:22:03</u> Right, right. So, if he's going to bomb Brent Ashworth, because did Brent have anything to do with CFS[5] and that financial deal?

---

[5] CFS stands for Coordinated Financial Services. Gary Sheets was the owner, and Steve Christensen was a key figure in its operation. It was in major financial difficulty, and Steve Christensen was

George: 01:22:14 No, but realize the news media and didn't acknowledge CFS as one of the problems. Only the police department did. The newspapers were more hung up and *Salamander* than CFS or whatever it is. And so, Hofmann doesn't know what the police are doing. He just knows what the newspapers are telling them they're doing.

GT: 01:22:33 Okay. So, the newspapers are focusing on the Mormon forgeries. So that wasn't in the newspapers at all back then?

George: 01:22:33 CFS?

GT: 01:22:40 That it could have been a mafia hit or something because I've heard that.

George: 01:22:46 Nor for a few days, no. They were hung up. I mean, what's more significant to read: *Salamander* or bomb for mafia?

GT: 01:22:46 I don't know. Bomb for mafia sounds pretty good to me.

George: 01:22:56 Oh no, not in Utah. *Salamander* was very controversial and of course Steve Christensen, he was the one in charge of the *Salamander Letter*, because it authenticated in trying to sell it?

GT: 01:23:06 Well, and I know Curt said that when he talked to Mark that day, Mark was kind of like feeling Curt out, like "What did the media know?

GT: 01:23:22 And he says, Mark said, "It must have. Mark said it must have been a financial deal."

GT: 01:23:22   And Curt said, "Well, not necessarily."

George: 01:23:28   Oh, Mark said it must've been a financial [deal]?

GT: 01:23:28   Yeah.

George: 01:23:30   Okay. That was his intent that the news media didn't pick it up. And if you look at the newspapers at that time, it's all *Salamander*. There's a link between Christensen and *Salamander*.

George: 01:23:39   Hmm. Wow. Wow. So, was Gary Sheets a collector too? Or not really?

George: 01:23:39   No.

GT: 01:23:39   He wasn't at all.

George: 01:23:46   No, not to my knowledge.

GT: 01:23:50   Ok, that's just crazy. So, this whole bombing thing was just a stall tactic for this farmer who is going to come beat him up?

George: 01:23:59   That's what it seemed like. We know it was a stall factor because he wanted two days, so they can meet on the contract back there. So, the Antiquarian Society, they were going to vote to buy it. And he knew that. And Schiller & Wapner assured him it would sell for over a million bucks. So, if they can put it off until the vote was on Wednesday, that would give him the excuse that he needed to stall for a little time.

George: 01:24:26   Well, because he was also supposed to meet with the church officials the day of the third bomb about the McLellin Collection.

George: <u>01:24:34</u> I don't believe that.

GT: <u>01:24:35</u> You don't believe that? Oh really?

George: <u>01:24:37</u> No I don't. There were a lot of stories going around
                 there. There were a lot of stories. I've heard them over
                 the years. I'm not saying that's not true. Realize they
                 say, each investigator is working on different aspects.
                 But I've heard so many things that are rumors and I've
                 never heard it from the investigators. I've heard from
                 other people and I never heard them from the church
                 and I dealt with them for quite a while. I'm not saying
                 it wasn't gonna happen. I says, "I don't know about it,"
                 so I can't effectively speak about it.

Hofmann, Church Leaders, & the McLellin Collection

Introduction

As you can see from our previous conversations, Mark had a tangled web of interactions. In this next conversation with forensics expert George Throckmorton, we'll talk more about Mark's dealings with church leaders. What got Mark in hot water with church officials? Check out our conversation....

GT: 01:25:08   Well, we'll talk a little bit about this because from what I understand, at least from the book *Salamander*. So, it sounds like Mark had a lot of irons in the fire.

George: 01:25:08   Oh, he did.

GT: 01:25:23   So he's trying to sell *Oath of a Freeman* for a million dollars and that's being slower for whatever. He had promised the church he was going to sell them the *Salamander Letter*? No, not in the *Salamander*, the McLellin Collection. And so, I believe he was supposed to do that on, I want to say it was Monday that the first two bombs went off. And then I thought the church said that they wanted to still meet with him Tuesday. So, he had to meet. He had an appointment with, I believe it was Elder Oaks, Elder Pinnock. I don't remember who all.

George: 01:25:58   Elder Pinnock was the one that was dealing with him quite a bit.

GT: 01:26:00   Yeah. And so, so can you a little bit about what was the relationship between Mark Hofmann and Elder Pinnock?

George: 01:26:15   Business. Elder Pinnock had a history. In fact, I've known him. He was my wife's bishop when we got married and so I've known him. I knew him for a long time before this and he was, you know, as much a victim as anybody. What happened here, it's kind of interesting. On the McLellin Collection we're going to be talking about. About as far as the meetings with the church. I don't know. I don't know anything about them. It didn't give me any reason to be concerned one way or another. I had no interest in his dealings with the church. I really didn't. So, I'm ignorant on that. All I know is what was told [to] me, but as far as the McLellin Collection, he found a document which was a land deed. I gotta get diverted here on a tangent again. It's a land deed. There's an old theory called a Solomon Spalding theory. Are you aware that?

GT: 01:27:03   I am aware of that.

George: 01:27:13   Okay. But one of the problems, it's never been given much credibility. They think that Solomon Spalding wrote it.

GT: 01:27:13   Wrote the Book of Mormon.

George: 01:27:24   And Martin[6] just copied the Book of Mormon, but there was really no relationship between Solomon

---

[6] George was referring to Martin Harris, but he meant Sidney Rigdon. In a future interview with Steven Mayfield, you can see the forged land deed with Sidney Rigdon's forged signature.

Spalding and Joseph Smith that could be found. So, it's not given a whole lot of credit. I mean there's always people that bring it up, but my opinion is not given credit because they never met until too late, until this land deed showed up. And it's a land deed that was signed by Solomon Spalding and Martin Harris. So, it showed there was a relationship between Solomon Spalding and Martin Harris and the date was appropriate. And this is the document that Mark Hofmann showed Hugh Pinnock and Al Rust and some others, and he says this is part of the McLellin Collection.

George:	<u>01:28:10</u>	And the story I heard, and I don't know what the real story is because I heard a lot of stories, but after Joseph Smith died, McLellin broke into his office and stole a lot of things and then left for Texas or whatever. I don't know. That's what I heard.

GT:	<u>01:28:10</u>	Broke into who's office?

George:	<u>01:28:23</u>	Joseph Smith's office after he got killed, and stole a lot of documents that showed he was a crook or whatever. Yeah. And I hear a lot of stories too, and I'm not a historian, I don't know. But I do know that this document, he said it was part of the McLellin Collection and you can see it's damaging because it shows him in Solomon Spalding were together. And he [Hofmann] got $186,000 loan on the basis of showing that to Hugh Pinnock and said this is part of the McLellin Collection and there's other damaging documents too.

George: <u>01:28:53</u>   And I understand he also showed it to a couple of others and got some more money. So, he was double-dipping. He was really. He played everybody against everybody there. And so, this document, which I later got and authenticated and found out he changed the date at the top. The land deed was correct. Except he changed the date and he also put it in the name of Solomon Spalding. Other than that, it was genuine. Oh, and Martin Harris, he put in the name of Solomon Spalding and Martin Harris. It was a land deed for I think Alma or Elma Spaulding or something like that. But if you have a witness, Solomon Spalding at the bottom and Martin Harris there, those signatures were both added, and the date was modified. So, you know, a genuine document except for those things. And of course, that's what made it valuable.

George: <u>01:29:42</u>   And so that was the basis of the McLellin Collection. And he said there's a lot of other damaging evidence too. And so, it's very controversial and so I don't know who he would have been meeting with at the church. I mean, I'm not saying. Again, I don't know, but I do know that that was it. Now, later on, on the McLellin Collection, I found when I went through the room down in the basement of the police department, when I first entered the case, I found a whole box full of documents signed by McMillan not McLellin, McMillan. And I just read through them and they're historical documents from 1800. He had a lot of these things. I don't know whether they were valuable, I don't know who McMillan was or anything else, but all he would've had to have done would be to change two letters and they wouldn't now be the McLellin Collection instead of the McMillan Collection.

George: 01:30:32   And that's something that he did. So, I could see a work in progress. I mean the missing 116 pages. He'd been working on that for two years and he did a whole lot of research on that from syntax analysis and so forth and etc. He was ready to go. He knew the names of the books and had a picture of how big they were and stuff like that. He had so many irons in the fire. I think that was his trip up. It was so easy for him to make money. He just kept doing it more and more and more and he couldn't keep everything straight. So, I'm not sure on that meeting with the church.

GT: 01:31:16   Yeah, and for the people who are listening to this, from what I understand was he had a meeting, because he had, he gotten a big loan that Hugh Pinnock had authorized at First Interstate Bank, and then the loan came due and he hadn't paid it back. So, the church was putting a lot of pressure on him. I know Curt Bench said that Mark was very hard to get ahold of, and so Steve Christensen had come and said, "Hey, you're going to be in a lot of trouble with the church if you don't pay this loan," and that sort of thing. So, it sounds like there was a lot of financial pressures he's getting. He's got these pressures from the *Oath of the Freeman*. He's getting pressures from McLellin, because he hasn't delivered. Apparently, this farmer; it sounds like it's a multifaceted thing.

George: 01:32:09   Well it was. He was getting a lot. Ironically, went down to she Brent Ashworth on Sunday and Brent was chewing him out because he, one of his checks bounced and so he wrote him out another check which also bounced.

GT: 01:32:17   Oh my goodness.

George: 01:32:19   See, that's Mark. He didn't care because nobody ever physically assaulted him. The church isn't going to send out the Danites[7] to kill him. Porter Rockwell's not around anymore and you know, they can threaten him and all that other stuff. It didn't matter, but he is getting pressure and he's getting it from many sources because he's been double-dipping. He's been like, again, the McLellin Collection, he sold the rights to that to two different people for over $100,000, so, a lot of pressure. But then when somebody hits him, that's the cork off the bottle, it suddenly explodes. He's not gonna take anymore. And it all happened within that period of time, yes.

GT: 01:32:56   Okay. So, Brent was giving them a lot of grief. Steve was given them some grief.

George: 01:33:00   Al Rust was given him some grief. The church has given him some grief.

GT: 01:33:04   I mean this three by five card. Was that kind of a hit list?

George: 01:33:08   Well, that's what we suspect. We found that in his belongings. He never addressed it. That was totally speculation on our part. We thought, well, why are

---

[7] Danites were an early Mormon militia group that often went after dissenters in the Nauvoo Period (1840s.)

his five friends on that card and why is Steve Christensen's name have the asterisk by it? And why was Steve the one blown up?

GT: 01:33:24   He was the only one that had the concrete nails in his bomb too. Is there a significance to that?

George: 01:33:29   Oh yeah, because that'll kill somebody. Again, he wanted to go to his funeral. So, he had to make sure he was dead.

GT: 01:33:37   And so he didn't.

George: 01:33:38   The others he didn't care about.

GT: 01:33:40   He was just fine with injuring them, although I guess Kathy died anyway.

George: 01:33:45   Well yes, she died. But again, he didn't care whether she picked it up or anybody picked up. If they would have seen the package and the driveway, which was by the car. And if they would've called the police and the police would come up and says, "Boy, you're lucky. You've got a bomb here." It would have still given the link between the two for the police to follow up on the investigation. Unfortunately, she picked it up and that's what caused the bomb. And with Brent Ashworth, again, it's a bomb. It doesn't matter whether it kills him or not, it's an excuse for him to go into hiding. So, the motives have changed a little bit.

GT: 01:34:21   And so he called this farmer that same day of the bomb, and said, "I got to go to a funeral?"

George: 01:34:30   We're not absolutely sure. I'm not. But I believe that's true. Again, I never spoke to him. He actually came to my house once. I got the privilege at 10:30 at night.

GT: 01:34:30   The farmer, you're talking about.

George: 01:34:40   Yeah, they flew him down here and I was at home. That's where the lab was, down to my basement, my basement lab, Hofmann's basement lab. Both fooled the FBI's multistory lab. But anyway, he came down, I had the privilege, and I say that sarcastically, of coming in at 10:30 and walking out after looking at it and say, "Sir, I'm sorry you just wasted $100,000 on this piece of paper."

GT: 01:35:07   Oh boy, I bet that made him feel good.

George: 01:35:07   And then the investigator that brought him in, flew him back and I never saw him before. What I'm telling you is what the other investigators told me. I never interacted with the people very often. That's what I liked about it. I got out of the police department business and into the crime lab because I don't like talking to people that much. The ones I dealt with are mostly dead and they don't cause too much, you know, conversational problems. So, the information I'm giving you is what was relayed to me by the various investigators. I've considered myself kind of a spoke in a wheel. You've got a lot of investigators out here and they're all doing their piece and so forth, but they all come down and talk to me whenever it comes to a document and there's a lot of things I don't know about regarding the investigation that may not be related to the documents. But anything related to the documents, even the investigators don't know because I never shared it with all the investigators. And I was telling you about the hot tub.

GT:	01:35:07	Yeah, let's go there now.

George:	01:36:09	I got to show you a Mark was doing the same thing. He's like the hub and all these people around him. We were talking to one of the people that said Mark had a hot tub and he invited people over at times to get in the hot tub with their wives or whatever. I don't know. But they were telling us that one time, they knew that Mark knew President Hinckley because they were in the hot tub and the phone rang and Mark got out and went over and talked to him, talked on the phone for about 10 minutes and come over and said, "Oh that was President Hinckley. He was just calling me about some stuff." So, they all believed he knew him personally and knew his phone number. But when we researched that President Hinckley was over in Germany at the time. He wasn't even here.

George:	01:36:51	So it wasn't President Hinckley that called him. And when we talked to President Hinckley, he made the comment, he says, "Oh yeah, I know him. I seen him a couple of times, but I don't know anything about him." It wasn't until after the investigation and people started talking to him. He learned more about Mark Hofmann after the bombings than he knew beforehand. But Mark had everybody believe that he knew him personally and had his private number and all this other stuff. And that's the way he talked to each one of the people. And if you talk to the people, they'll each have their own theory and they'll think that Mark was telling the truth. We had one of the people that told us that he found the *Salamander Letter* and he was threatened and he was on the verge of being arrested when he finally said, "Oh no, I didn't find it. Mark did." And in fact, he was telling us the truth, but all he knew is what Mark told him. And he believed him. Everybody believes Mark.

GT: 01:36:51 Wow.

George: 01:37:50 He was a good con artist.

GT: 01:37:53 Yes, He was excellent at it.

Why Didn't Hofmann Get Harsher Sentence?

Introduction

Given all the mounting evidence against Mark Hofmann, why were prosecutors interested in a plea deal? It seems evidence was pretty strong to convict him of a 1st Degree murder. George Throckmorton tells of conversations between prosecutors and Hofmann's lawyers. Check out our conversation....

GT: 01:37:55   What I understand is Mark Hofmann pleaded guilty to second degree murder and it seems like at least, you know, I'm not an investigator, but it seems like he probably should've gotten first degree. There's a lot of premeditation going on and things like that. So why was there a plea bargain? You know, and I know he's gotten a big stiff sentence anyway, even with second degree murder. Well, why did we plea bargain to second degree murder on this?

George: 01:38:25   Politics. It has always intrigued me. The amount of politics that takes place in everything, criminal investigations are the same thing. I remember that Ted Cannon was the county attorney at that time, district attorney, and it was his feelings that any high-profile case should go to court, and he was a firm believer in that. One of the prosecutors, however, is known for liking to make plea bargains. It's easier. It's simpler. You get a conviction and that's really all that matters, sometimes. There was a meeting that took place that I was present to and two other people were present to also.

George: 01:39:19   Before I get there, I forgot. Ted Cannon, in the process of the investigation was so valuable. He was a printer before he became an attorney. So, he gave us a lot of information on printed documents that were counterfeited and forged. And again, it was his belief to go to court. So, the public would be aware of all of the evidence. However, he got involved in a scandal in his office and he resigned early. The new district attorney volunteered to come in early to take care of the office because he had won the election but hadn't been sworn in yet. So, he volunteered to come in early and I met with him the day after he took office with one of the other attorneys and he made the comment at the time, he said, "George, this is not my investigation. It's costing a lot of money. We don't have the funds. I want it to end." And he instructed the other attorney, "Go out and make a deal and get this off the plate so we can get to our normal routine." And then he turned to me and he said, "George, as soon as we get a plea, as soon as we get a conviction, you're going to be out of a job. We no longer need you here.

George: 01:40:42   Now the irony of that, I guess as I had worked for the attorney general's office to assist them with the case and after six months of assisting them, they called me in and said, "We're not here to pay your salary to work for another agency. You've got to quit and come back and work for us. We've got work for you to do here." And I went and talked to Ted Cannon and told him that and he says, "We need you here. The investigation is going to last at least another

year and we can't do it without you. You're the only
document examiner that knows these things. And so,
he offered me a job. He says, "If you quit the
attorney general's office and I'll hire you down here."

GT: 01:40:42   Down here, meaning?

George: 01:41:29   The district attorney's office, and so I had a decision
to make. Do I stay with the attorney general and quit
the Hofmann case, or do I stick with a Hofmann case
through completion, which was still going to be
several more months that I knew of?

George: 01:41:46   I had looked at over 600 documents during that
period of time and although they were not going to
be brought in the trial, it was still important for the
overall investigation and the evidence and I'm the
only one that could do it. It's awful to be in that
situation, but honestly nobody but me and Bill Flynn
knew what we were doing, and Bill was in Arizona,
so I made a decision. I resigned from the attorney
general's office and was hired at the district
attorney's office and then it was like three months
later, maybe four months later was when Ted left,
and the new district attorney called me in and told
me I was going to be laid off as soon as Hofmann
pled guilty. So, the follow-up is, I was laid off on
Valentine's Day, in fact, six years from retirement
and had to start all over again.

George: 01:42:41   I was a little frustrated on that. In fact, I had to go to
San Diego because there was no job here for me at
the time. So that's why the deal was made. The
district attorney made the decision. He didn't want
to continue the investigation, which was costing a lot

of money. I know a lot of people have speculated about how the church was involved and we didn't want to call witnesses to the stand and all that other stuff. That's just total bologna and that's the nicest word I can use. The wonderful thing about that investigative team that I really liked. We had a couple of good Mormons, if you will. We had a couple of anti-Mormons, if you will. We had some attorneys that wanted to fight. We had attorneys that wanted to deal. We had a diversity of people and we had a lot of discussions.

George: 01:43:27   We had a lot of disagreements. You talked about the plea bargain that was made. In my opinion and the opinion of most of the investigators there, it wasn't handled properly at all. But because there was instructions made to settle the case period, it was settled before it should have been. And for instance, it's normal in law enforcement if ever you make a plea bargain. The purpose is you get the confession from the person first and if that person cooperates, then you go in and recommend the plea bargain because if you made the plea bargain first, the suspect has no reason to cooperate and that's exactly what happened with Mark Hofmann.

GT: 01:44:13   Hmm.

George: 01:44:15   They made the deal before he was interviewed and although the transcript of the interview I think is so thick, three to four inches thick. In fact, maybe even two books, I can't remember. The parts I read through, they're not 100 percent accurate. Some of them are outright lies, but who knows the difference? And see, for instance, the stipulation was that when Hofmann was to confess officially that I would be present whenever we talked about the forgeries; that the homicide investigators would be present whenever he talked about the homicides; the fraud investigators would be present, when he talked about his fraudulent activities. That never happened. In fact, I was fired before he even had his confession and so I was not even allowed to talk to him. But one of the attorneys that was there would come out to me and talk to me afterwards and said, as an example, just as an example, he said, "Mark said that he got the paper from the *Salamander Letter* in a book up with the University of Utah, called such and such." I went up there. Book wasn't there. There was no pages taken out of it. It's just an outright lie. Now, whether he intentionally lied or whether he just forgot because he's dealing in so many different documents, I don't know. I'll give him the benefit of the doubt, but I do know that many of the things that he said were inaccurate. They were not true.

GT: 01:45:43   In his confession?

George: 01:45:43   In his confession.

GT: 01:45:44   Hmm.

George: 01:45:46   But it was handled wrong. But in retrospect, looking back at it, I do not criticize the attorneys that I disagreed with because as we look back, because he did confess, the FBI had to admit that they were forged and other people had to admit that he was a crook instead of an honest guy that we were framing, if you will. So overall it turned out okay. But the accusations as to why are totally wrong. The *L.A. Times*, for instance, would talk about how the church was hiding documents all the time. They did. What we found out is Mark Hofmann was their secret snitch. He was feeding them that because it would escalate the price of a document if it was controversial. They talk about the way the church hid documents. It just didn't happen. The one document President Hinckley hid. He didn't hide it. He was running the church in that time.

George: 01:46:50   He was overseas. He was doing so many things. He was working towards it, but the way they can distort things and the way they distorted the plea bargain, it was handled wrong in my humble opinion. But the results turned out okay, and Hofmann killed himself, if you will, when he went in the parole board and they recommended that he be there without possibility of parole because otherwise he could have been given parole. Hofmann's attorney said, "This is a first-degree murder. They're going to execute him." And that's why he was willing to plea bargain too. So, it's a complicated issue, but a lot of politics are involved anytime there's a plea bargain.

GT: 01:47:43   If you had, if you could see Mark today, what questions would you want to ask him?

George: 01:47:43   Quite frankly, none.

GT: 01:47:43   None?

George: 01:47:50   I have no desire to see him. If I were to talk to him, he would lie to me anyway because he always did. I think he's a pathological liar. I'm certain. I mean he passed the polygraph machine up at the university, and that's an interesting story there because the professor up there and didn't believe in the polygraph. He started researching it to write an article. He became a believer and became a polygraph examiner. And then Hofmann went up there and he passed with flying colors. Well, we know that because he's, he's a psychopathic liar and he doesn't have any emotion. His family didn't know what he was doing. He could hide it from everybody. His parents, they didn't know what he was doing. They believed him 100 percent. He could lie to everybody. And if I were to talk to him, I don't know whether he would tell me his real name.

GT:	01:48:34	How do you think you passed that polygraph test?

George:	01:48:36	Because he's a pathological liar. And if you are, you can pass any polygraph. If you think you're telling the truth or if you don't. See polygraphs. Interesting thing on polygraph. I was working with the guy in Ogden who for five years that did it. We talked daily, every day and we would compare notes. There was actually some research done on polygraph years ago back in the sixties where they hooked it up to a plant. I don't know if you heard about that or not. They hooked the polygraph up to a plant and the plant emits emotions which can be detected on the polygraph. It's an interesting story. You ought to read it sometime and there's a movie on tv called *Mythbusters*.

GT:	01:48:36	I love *Mythbusters*.

George: <u>01:49:24</u> They duplicated that about three years ago, modified, but they duplicated it. They found the same results. You hook that polygraph machine up to a plant and when a dog walks in the room, it goes wild. They had a caretaker that went in and cut his finger. The instance he cut his finger, the plant responded because that was the person that would talk to the plant and water the plant and so forth. The polygraph is very sensitive, but if you don't have a conscience it doesn't work.

GT: <u>01:49:53</u> Wow. So, is that why they won't allow that as evidence in court?

George: <u>01:50:00</u> More or less, more or less. It's not a hundred percent true because of the weakness of the polygraph operator. The machine Is accurate. It's how it's interpreted that causes problems in the courtroom. Just like history, how it's interpreted. I mean, I go to an accident scene to do a reconstruction of an accident and you have five witnesses and all tell a different story. Are they lying? No, but they don't see the same thing. It's from a different angle depending upon their past history is how they'll interpret it.

George: <u>01:50:39</u> And so what you do, and that's why I like what I'm doing and you get all of their stories, put them together and then it's like the pieces of a puzzle and you put them together and see what's more logical. Is it 100 percent? Even DNA isn't 100 percent forensic science. Do you know what the word forensic means?

GT: <u>01:50:56</u> I used to know, but I can't remember.

George: <u>01:50:56</u>   Debate.

GT: <u>01:50:56</u>   Debate.

George: <u>01:51:00</u>   But because of a television program called *Quincy*, forensic pathologist, it changed the whole meaning of the word. It now means the scientific examination of evidence.

GT: <u>01:51:12</u>   Because of a tv show?

George: <u>01:51:14</u>   But it is forensic because it's debated in the courtroom. That's why you can always have opposing witnesses, even documents. The study that's been done on handwriting examination when you're properly trained is still only 96.4 percent accurate.

GT: <u>01:51:30</u>   So is it true that you can figure out a person's characteristics just based on the way they write?

George: <u>01:51:35</u>   Sure. You can find out too, by the way, the moons in the sky and the stars are in the sky. NOT! {chuckles}

George: <u>01:51:44</u>   I did some research years ago which was published, which shows it is just baloney. I sent four different writings to a well-known graphologist in Chicago, except I changed the name. One was a woman, one was a man, one was 25, one was 64 and they came back with contradictory traits and it's the same handwriting they examined, so it's not a scientific analysis. It's whatever they do, I don't know.

GT: <u>01:51:44</u>   Like fortune telling.

George: 01:52:12   That's absolutely true. I didn't want to use that term, but yes.

GT: 01:52:16   Wow. Wow. Alright. Well I really appreciate you taking the time to talk with us here on *Gospel Tangents*. I may have to schedule another interview about Howard Hughes though. Maybe the Hi-Fi Murders too.

George: 01:52:31   I'll tell you this. In my career I've worked in various places. I've been in Chicago, in Washington, and San Diego, and Salt Lake and Ogden, and it has been the most fascinating life that anybody could experience. I've met with some of the smartest people in the professional organizations: The American Academy of Forensic Science, American Academy of Science, the International Association. There's thousands of members from all around the world and I sit next to the scientists and somebody will be talking about evolution as an example and I'll be sitting next to the people. I don't know anything about it, but I'm talking to the people that do and they'll say, "That's not true. He's using the wrong equation here. They're using the wrong elements," and they're both arguing against each other. But what gets published? The guy that makes the presentation, and I think that's why I enjoy it so much because these are men of science. And James Talmage, one of my favorite, well known scientist that's a member of the church in one of his books, he said, "a theory is there until eventually it's changed to a new theory. And that stays in effect until it's changed to a new theory." And I've given presentations at times over the years. And I say there's two things I don't depend on. One is science and one is history. The three things I like or

magic, movies, and professional wrestling. You can
depend on that because you get what you expect.
But I believe that 100 percent.

GT: 01:52:31   That's great.

George: 01:54:09   But I appreciate you asking me to talk. It's been my
privilege.

GT: 01:54:11   Yeah, it's been great. Before I let you go, are there
any other really high-profile cases that you worked
on besides the ones that we've already mentioned?

George: 01:54:20   What do you want? Lafferty's?

GT: 01:54:22   Lafferty's. You worked on that one?

George: 01:54:31   Hi Fi Shop, again, Howard Hughes. What's the other
one?   Guys you don't know of. Redmond his name
for $173,000,000 in Nevada, Shakespeare, the guy
who wrote Shakespeare. That's enough.

GT: 01:54:31   Elizabeth Smart?

George: 01:54:47   Oh, I was a director of the lab when that happened.
That was a fiasco and that was our fault.

GT: 01:54:55   That's interesting.

George: 01:54:57   That's an interesting story which shouldn't have
happened, but again, politics get involved. We could
have done better, I'll put it that way. We could have
done a whole lot better with the crime scene portion
of it. In Ogden when we went to the Hi-Fi Shop, for
instance, it's a smaller organization so we could do
things that they can't do here because of

bureaucracy. When we went to a crime scene, we would have an investigator. We would have a crime scene specialist, and we would have an attorney, so we would know from the beginning to the end what we needed and we could work.

George: 01:55:39 Here, no. The investigators come and keep out the crime lab till they're through. Then the crime lab comes, and they don't talk to the investigators and the attorneys never get involved until several weeks later and it causes fiasco. It could be handled a lot better.

GT: 01:55:49 Wow. That's interesting. Mark Hacking? Were you involved in that at all?

George: 01:55:49 No.

GT: 01:55:56 No. Okay, so I finally found one that you missed.

George: 01:55:59 Which one was that? Remind me.

GT: 01:56:01 He was the one he murdered his wife.

George: 01:56:03 Yes, the only way we got involved on that is one of our guys found the body and the dump.

GT: 01:56:09 It was terrible.

George: 01:56:10 But no, we didn't know we didn't get involved in it. I think that was the sheriff, if I recall it. I can't remember, but we didn't.

GT: 01:56:20 Okay, well, once again, George Throckmorton. Thank you for this interesting, fascinating look into in the

Mark Hofmann and like I said, I might have to call you again. Thank you for letting me be here.

George: <u>01:56:26</u>   Alright.

George: <u>01:56:31</u>   You're supposed to say "Cut!"

Figure 1 - George Throckmorton (retired SLPD) on how he figured out how Mark Hofmann was forging documents. He previously worked in the Attorney General's Office at the State of Utah. © Copyright 2018 - Gospel Tangents

Additional Resources

If you are interested in the Hofmann bombings and forgeries, check out our other interviews.

Figure 2 - Shannon Flynn describes working with Mark Hofmann. © Copyright 2017 - Gospel Tangents

088: **Christmas Party Plea Deal** (Flynn)
https://wp.me/p8l6gx-kc

087: **Mark's Unusual Prison Visitors** (Flynn)
https://gospeltangents.com/2017/10/19/mark-hofmanns-unusual-prison-visitors/

086: **Would Hofmann Kill Again?** (Flynn)
https://gospeltangents.com/2017/10/15/would-mark-hofmann-kill-again/

085: **Should Hofmann Ever Be Released from Prison?** (Flynn)
https://gospeltangents.com/2017/10/13/mark-hofmann-in-prison/

084: **Shannon Goes to Jail for Hofmann** (Flynn)
https://gospeltangents.com/2017/10/11/shannon-flynn-jailed-hofmanns-crimes/

083: Hofmann's Last Bomb Blew the Lid off Mormon History (Flynn)
https://gospeltangents.com/2017/10/09/hofmanns-last-bomb-blew-lid-off-mormon-history/

082: Hoffman's Best Fake: Fooling the Lie Detector Test (Flynn)
https://gospeltangents.com/2017/10/04/hofmanns-best-fake-fooling-lie-detector-test/

081: Mark's Million-Dollar Con (Flynn)
https://gospeltangents.com/2017/10/01/marks-million-dollar-con/

080: "I Cheat People. That's What I do for a Living." (Flynn)
https://gospeltangents.com/2017/09/30/personality-master-forger/

079: Hofmann's Teenage Forgeries (Flynn)
https://wp.me/p8l6gx-j6

SANDRA TANNER - MORMON CRITIC'S VIEW OF MARK HOFMANN

Figure 3 - Sandra Tanner - Utah Lighthouse Ministries on interactions with Mark Hofmann. © Copyright 2018 - Gospel Tangents

177: How Jerald Tanner Identified Fake Salamander Letter (Tanner)
https://gospeltangents.com/2018/07/21/how-jerald-tanner-identified-fake-salamander-letter/

176: When Mark Hofmann met Sandra Tanner (Tanner)
https://gospeltangents.com/2018/07/19/when-mark-hofmann-met-sandra-tanner-part-1/

036: **Bombs in Salt Lake: Introduction to Mark Hofmann**
See
https://wp.me/p8l6gx-bs
Video:
https://youtu.be/hxC12GXE5Ws

Figure 4 - Curt Bench, Owner of Benchmark Books & key witness in Hofmann Forgery & Bombing Case. © Copyright 2017 - Gospel Tangents

037: **White Salamander Letter & Other Forgeries**
https://wp.me/p8l6gx-bU
Video: https://youtu.be/qCt4v47KMlc

038: **Bomb Day 1: 2 Killed – October 15, 1985**
https://wp.me/p8l6gx-bX
Video: https://youtu.be/SaVSHcFtr8k

039: **Bomb Day 2: Other Targets? October 16, 1985**
https://wp.me/p8l6gx-ca
Video: https://youtu.be/ars8PDjDAto

040: **Curt Bench's role in Hofmann Bombings Court Case**
https://wp.me/p8l6gx-cf
Video: https://youtu.be/QS0Spyc497Q

041: **Should LDS Leaders have Detected Hofmann's Fraud?**
https://wp.me/p8l6gx-cl
Video: https://youtu.be/n0q4G5zZKdY

042: **Hofmann Bombings Effects on Mormon History**
https://wp.me/p8l6gx-cz
 Video: https://youtu.be/6Y3eoZlXPv8

Epilogue

I hope you enjoyed our conversation with George Throckmorton. It was really fun. I hope you enjoyed it as much as I did. Thanks George! Really, it was a lot of fun.

For those of you who are interested in a transcript of the entire interview, go to www.GospelTangents.com/shop and I will send you one right away. So, if you subscribe for just $10 a month, on our website, I will send you this and all other future transcripts as soon as they're available. You can also go to our Amazon page and find all of our transcripts if you're interested in more of a paperback version of these. So, check it out. And thanks again for listening.

- A paperback version of the transcript is available on our Amazon page: https://amzn.to/2MocT3E
- Make sure that you like our page on www.facebook.com/GospelTangents.
- You can subscribe at YouTube, at www.youtube.com/GospelTangents.
- We're also on Twitter @GospelTangents
- For entire interviews, go to www.Patreon.com/GospelTangents
- as well as make sure that you subscribe on Apple Podcasts so you don't miss any of our episodes.